A **WHERE'S WALLY?**
FUN FACT BOOK

FIGHTING KNIGHTS

Based on the characters created by

MARTIN HANDFORD

WRITTEN BY RACHEL WRIGHT

WALKER BOOKS

AND SUBSIDIARIES

LONDON • BOSTON • SYDNEY

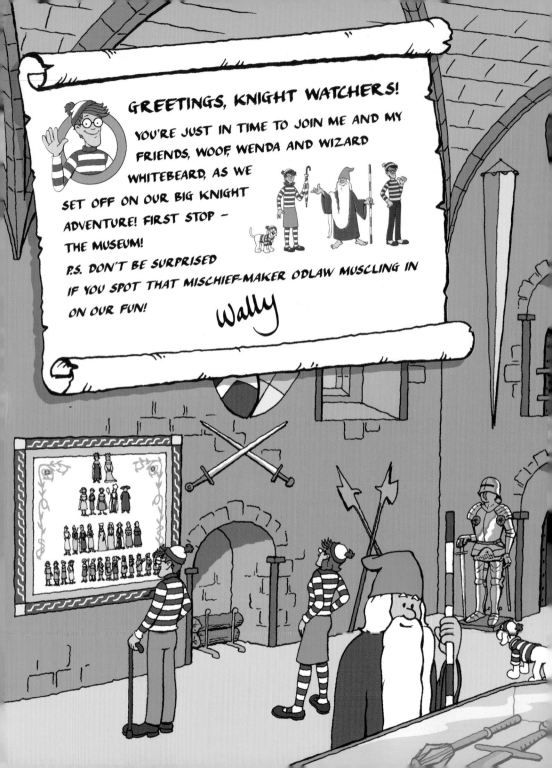

KNIGHT TIMES

Knights were warriors trained to fight on horseback. They lived in Europe long ago, during a time called the Middle Ages. This lasted from about 700 to 1500. Powerful knights, who were also great lords, fought for a king or emperor. Less powerful knights might also be nobles, but fought for a great lord, instead. To pay them for their fighting, knights were often given land to live on and farm.

King   Queen

Great Lords   Bishops

Knights   Priests

Serfs   More Serfs

The most powerful people in the Middle Ages were kings and emperors. Next in line came top churchmen, great lords and other nobles. At the bottom were poor workers called serfs. In return for a knight's protection, they farmed his land and did all the muckiest chores.

FIGHTING FASHION

Galloping garters! Wally's gone back to the 1200s to help a knight get dressed! At first, knights wore armour made from linked metal rings called mail. Underneath they wore a padded coat to soften heavy blows from enemy weapons.

Metal helmet had narrow eye slits and small breathing holes.

Padded cap worn underneath a helmet helped soften blows to the head.

To clean off rust, mail armour was shaken about in a sack containing sand and vinegar.

Padded coat helped stop the mail from rubbing and cutting into the knight's skin.

Mail stockings were tied to a belt underneath the padded coat.

Pointed spurs helped the knight make his horse gallop.

Cloth surcoat helped keep the sun's heat off the mail beneath.

Palms of mail mittens were made of leather, to improve the knight's grip.

MAN IN A CAN

Mail protected against sword cuts, but it didn't protect against arrows and spears. So, in time, knights began covering bits of their bodies with pieces of steel called plates. Gradually, more and more plates were added.

Mail armour with steel plates, 1360.

By the 1400s, knights were covered from top to toe in plate armour. Most of the plates overlapped each other, like a lobster shell. They were joined together on the inside by straps, or by sliding or pivoting fastenings, so that the knight could bend his body.

Plate armour, 1480. With plate armour, knights no longer needed shields.

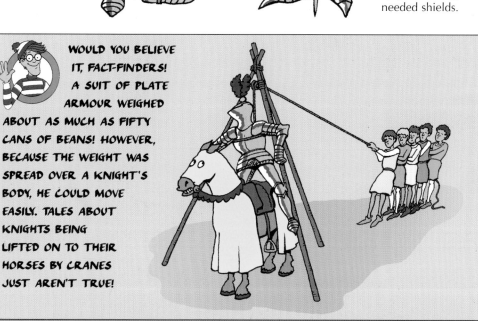

WOULD YOU BELIEVE IT, FACT-FINDERS! A SUIT OF PLATE ARMOUR WEIGHED ABOUT AS MUCH AS FIFTY CANS OF BEANS! HOWEVER, BECAUSE THE WEIGHT WAS SPREAD OVER A KNIGHT'S BODY, HE COULD MOVE EASILY. TALES ABOUT KNIGHTS BEING LIFTED ON TO THEIR HORSES BY CRANES JUST AREN'T TRUE!

BOLD BATTLERS

Suffering swordsmen! Wally and Woof have stumbled across a battle! No knight worth his spurs ignored a call to arms from his king or lord – although some knights paid money instead of fighting. Often, big battles began with a charge by knights on horseback. Each knight had a heavy spear, or lance, tucked under one arm, which he used to knock down the enemy. Fingers crossed these leading lancers don't mow down our friends!

SITTING STEADY

Long stirrups and a high-backed saddle helped a knight fight without falling off his horse. Stirrups were invented in China way back in the 500s. They didn't become popular in Europe until the early Middle Ages.

NABBED KNIGHTS

Believe it or not, knights often tried *not* to kill enemy knights in battle. Instead, defeated knights were held captive until their friends or family paid for them to be set free. A champion knight could make a lot of money if he captured the right enemy!

WICKED WEAPONS

After charging into battle, a knight dropped his lance and used one of his other weapons. Sometimes he fought on foot, too.

Heavy lance, 1100s
Ideal for knocking an enemy off his horse. Light lances could be used for stabbing overarm or throwing.

Pollaxe, 1400s
Just the thing for bashing an enemy over the head, especially when fighting on foot.

Flat, double-edged sword, 1200s
Good for slashing and slicing.

Very pointed sword, 1400s
Developed for thrusting through gaps in plate armour.

Metal-topped mace, 1400s
Perfect for dashing an enemy's brains out.

Dagger, 1400s Handy for stabbing someone close by.

GOOD KNIGHTS, BAD KNIGHTS

During the Middle Ages a set of rules for knights was formed. These rules were called chivalry. They were incredibly hard to stick to!

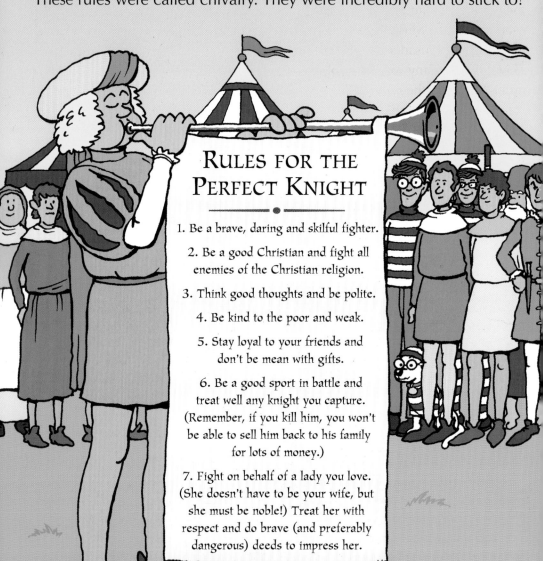

RULES FOR THE PERFECT KNIGHT

1. Be a brave, daring and skilful fighter.

2. Be a good Christian and fight all enemies of the Christian religion.

3. Think good thoughts and be polite.

4. Be kind to the poor and weak.

5. Stay loyal to your friends and don't be mean with gifts.

6. Be a good sport in battle and treat well any knight you capture. (Remember, if you kill him, you won't be able to sell him back to his family for lots of money.)

7. Fight on behalf of a lady you love. (She doesn't have to be your wife, but she must be noble!) Treat her with respect and do brave (and preferably dangerous) deeds to impress her.

CRUEL CRUSADERS

Many knights tried to prove they were good Christians by going on crusades. Crusades were trips to the eastern Mediterranean to fight followers of the Muslim religion. Sadly, not all crusaders behaved chivalrously. Many were horribly cruel, and used the crusades to steal loot and gain great glory for themselves.

NOBLE KNIGHTS

Stories about knights and chivalry became popular during the Middle Ages. The most famous tells the legend of King Arthur and his knights. Together, they sat at a huge round table and made plans to fight baddies. Odlaw, are you sure you're at the right table?

WARIN OF WALCOTE WAS ONE NASTY KNIGHT! WHEN TOLD HE COULDN'T MARRY THE LADY HE LOVED, HE WENT TO HER HOUSE AND KIDNAPPED HER! SEE IF YOU CAN SPOT HIM SOMEWHERE IN THIS BOOK. HE HAS A SMALL STRAIGHT SCAR ON HIS FACE.

KNIGHT SCHOOL

Becoming a knight wasn't easy. By the late Middle Ages, only sons of noblemen were allowed to train for the job – which took ten years or more. All in all, it was a long and pricey process.

At about seven years old, a knight-to-be was sent to a relative's castle … without his mum or dad!

There, he learned how to ride, use weapons and behave politely. He also worked as a page, serving at dinner and doing odd jobs.

A page learnt to use a lance by charging at a wooden target. He had to hit the middle of the shield on the target's crossbar …

without getting thumped by the sandbag on the other end. Looks like Odlaw could do with a bit more practice!

At about fourteen, a page became a squire. He had to help an experienced knight and follow him into battle.

Once a squire was eighteen or older, he was ready to be knighted. He spent the night before his knighting ceremony in church, praying.

The next day, he knelt before another knight who tapped him on the neck or shoulders with his hand or sword.

Finally, he was given his sword and spurs, which showed that he had at last become a knight.

HEY THERE, HISTORY HOUNDS! NOT EVERYONE WAS KNIGHTED IN SUCH A GRAND WAY. IN THE EARLY DAYS, SOME MEN WERE MADE KNIGHTS ON THE BATTLEFIELD. A KNIGHT SIMPLY TAPPED THEM ON THE SHOULDERS WITH HIS HAND OR SWORD. INCREDIBLE! HOW MANY SWORDS CAN YOU SPOT ON THESE TWO PAGES?

JOLLY JOUSTS

Leaping lances! Our four friends have been invited to a joust!
A joust was a competition between two knights on horseback.

WAR GAMES

Jousts often took place at fancy events called tournaments. Mock battles and fights on foot were fought at tournaments, too. Mock battles were fun fights between two teams of knights armed with lances and swords. Each knight tried to capture as many opponents as possible. The captured knights then had to pay to be set free.

HEY, WALLY WATCHERS! DID YOU KNOW THAT A COAT OF ARMS CONTAINS NO MORE THAN FIVE COLOURS - BLUE, RED, GREEN, BLACK AND PURPLE - AND TWO METALS - GOLD (YELLOW) AND SILVER (WHITE)? A STRICT RULE IS THAT A COLOUR CAN NEVER BE PLACED ON TOP OF ANOTHER COLOUR. HAVE YOU SPOTTED AN ODD SHIELD THAT BREAKS THESE LAWS?

WILLIAM
MOWBRAY

Each knight charged towards the other and tried to knock him off his horse, or to break his lance on his shield. Ladies often came to watch their favourite knight jousting. Once, a woman was even offered as a prize! Let's hope no one tries to award Wenda to the winner!

PERSONAL PATTERNS

Knights at tournaments were recognized by the colours and patterns that decorated their clothes, shields and flags. These patterns are called coats of arms because knights sometimes wore them on their surcoats. Each family had its own coat of arms. When a father died, his family's coat of arms was passed on to his eldest son.

PETER, BISHOP
OF WINCHESTER

ROBERT
DE ROS

WILLIAM
LORD BOTREAUX

MICHAEL
DE LA POLE

FUN DAYS AND KNIGHTS

When they weren't busy bashing each other with lances and swords, noble knights loved to go hunting. The animals they caught, such as birds, boar and deer, were tasty to eat. And galloping around the countryside was good training for war. Sometimes noble women went hunting too. Unlike men, however, they usually rode side-saddle – with both legs on the same side of the horse. Steady on that saddle, Wenda!

PAMPERED PETS

Knights used special breeds of dog to help them hunt down boar, wolves and deer. Like Woof, hunting dogs were well looked after. Some even had heated kennels!

FOOD FACTS

Like other people in the Middle Ages, knights often ate off large pieces of stale bread instead of plates. After a meal, the bread was either eaten or given to the poor or the dogs. Just think how much washing-up this saved!

FUN AND GAMES

In their spare time, knights liked to sing, dance and play games such as dice and chess. Chess was often played for money, which led to arguments. It is said that King John of England once got so cross during a game of chess, he smashed the board over his opponent's head. Ouch!

 DID YOU KNOW THAT KNIGHTS USED TRAINED FALCONS TO CATCH BIRDS, RABBITS AND HARES? SOME OF THE FALCONS WERE SPOILED ROTTEN! THEY HAD PERCHES IN THEIR OWNERS' BEDROOMS, AND WERE FED BETTER FOOD THAN MOST POOR PEOPLE.

HUGE HOMES

Have you ever explored a castle? In the Middle Ages a castle was a fort, house, army camp and business centre all rolled into one! It was the place where a powerful lordly knight lived with his family, servants and soldiers. It was also where the knight's officials organized his farms, collected his rents and judged crimes. Some castles may even have had a dreadful dungeon where prisoners could be kept.

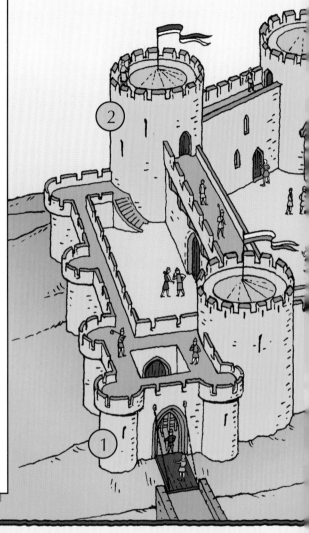

FROM STICKS TO STONES

The first castles were usually made from wood and earth. They were quick to put up but easy to burn down, so later castles were made from stone. Early stone castles were built around a strong main tower called a keep.

Castle made from wood and earth, 1000s

1. **Gatehouse** – protected the entrance to the castle. It had a drawbridge which was pulled up by chains and a portcullis (iron grille) which could be dropped in front of the door.

2. **Towers** – were used for defence. They also had rooms for sleeping and storage.

3. **Great hall** – the main room in the castle. It was used for all important events.

4. **Kitchen** – joined to the great hall by a passageway.

5. **Workshops** – weapons, armour and horseshoes were all made here by the castle's clever craftsmen.

Stone castle with square keep, 1100s

Stone castle with two circles of walls, 1200s

CASTLE INSIDES

Suffering spells! Wizard Whitebeard's made a wall of a great hall disappear! The great hall was the main room in a castle. It was used by the knight for important meetings. It was also used for eating, feasting and sleeping. After supper, the dining tables were cleared away to make room for lots of straw mattresses which the servants slept on. Only the super-rich had their own bedrooms in the Middle Ages. So, it looks like our four friends will be sleeping on the floor!

COOL FOOD

Kitchens were originally built
away from the great hall because of
the risk of fire. But food got cold on its way
to the table, so later kitchens were built nearer to
the great hall. Rooms for keeping food, baking
bread, making beer, and storing wine were also
nearby. Drinking water came from the castle's well.

ONE ROOM FEW CASTLES HAD
WAS A BATHROOM! WHEN A
KNIGHT WANTED A BATH, HIS
SERVANTS FILLED A WOODEN
TUB WITH BUCKETS OF HEATED WATER.
HOW MANY BUCKETS CAN YOU FIND
HIDDEN ON THESE TWO PAGES?

MISSION: ATTACK AND DEFEND!

Attackers used all sorts of terrible tactics to capture a castle and its lands. One popular ploy was to camp outside a castle, letting no food in, and wait until the people inside starved. Another was to try and get in by force. Inside the castle, the defenders fought back furiously. They shot arrows at the attackers outside. They also hurled boiling water and rocks on to their heads.

1. Missile throwers – giant slings threw huge rocks and other missiles over the castle walls.

2. Battlements – designed to hide defenders while they reloaded their weapons.

3. Arrow loops – let castle archers shoot their arrows without being seen.

4. Battering ram – its iron tip could punch holes in walls and doors.

5. Mangonel – huge catapult powered by the tension of tightly twisted ropes.

WOBBLY WALLS

One way to break down a castle wall was to destroy it from below. Attackers dug a tunnel under the wall, propped it up with wooden posts, then set fire to the posts. The tunnel caved in, bringing down the wall with it.

GUESS WHAT, WALLY-WATCHERS! CASTLES DIDN'T HAVE FLUSH TOILETS. INSTEAD, THEY HAD CHUTES WHICH WERE BUILT INTO THE CASTLE'S WALLS. WEE AND OTHER WASTE DROPPED DOWN THE CHUTE AND OUT INTO A PIT OR MOAT BELOW. IN 1204 A CASTLE ATTACKER BROKE INTO A CASTLE BY CLIMBING UP A CHUTE. LET'S HOPE NO ONE WAS USING THE TOILET AT THE TIME!

NIGHT NIGHT, KNIGHTS!

As the Middle Ages went on, the way wars were fought changed. Rulers began hiring more and more soldiers who fought for money, rather than for land. And foot soldiers, armed with pikes, crossbows and guns, became more powerful in battle than knights with lances. Slowly but surely, the day of the knight came to an end.

KNIGHT KEBABS

By the late Middle Ages, foot soldiers were the most important part of an army. Some carried six metre long spears called pikes. A hedgehog of pikemen could skewer a charge of knights horribly.

FEEBLE FIRE

Knights in armour were no match for gunpowder. Gunpowder was first used in Europe in the 1300s. To begin with, guns loaded with gunpowder were as unreliable as Odlaw. Sometimes they even blew up in the gunner's face! In time, however, they became much more reliable … and much more deadly.

THE END OF CASTLES

Like knights, castles slowly fell out of fashion. This was partly because private wars between castle owners became less common, so fort-like homes were no longer needed. Also, when gunpowder and cannons became powerful, castles stopped being safe. Nowadays, all that is left of many castles are their lonely ruins.

THE FIGHTING KNIGHTS CHECKLISTS

CALLING ALL WHERE'S WALLY? TIME-TRAVELLERS! NOW
THAT YOU CAN TELL A LETHAL LANCE FROM A DEADLY
DAGGER, GALLOP BACK TO THE BEGINNING OF THE BOOK
AND START SEARCHING FOR ALL THESE KNIGHT-TIME THINGS.

KNIGHTS CHECKLIST

- Four fallen spurs
- Sixteen fluttering flags
- A closed book
- A lost horseshoe
- Nine stripy tents
- Two mighty maces
- A scary skull
- An open book
- A pink-eared mouse
- A burst wine barrel
- Sixteen horses
- A brown briefcase
- Five grey shaggy dogs
- A knight scratching his nose
- Three men with spades

LOST PROPERTY

Can you remember where you first spied these knightly knick-knacks?

FEUDAL FEATURES

All these faces appear in the book, but not exactly as they look here. Can you spot the differences?

ANSWERS

Good Knights, Bad Knights – Warin turns up in **Fun Days and Knights**.
Knight School – Nineteen steely swords and two wooden ones.
Jolly Jousts – Odlaw's shield in **Knight School** breaks this law.
Castle Insides – Three buckets.

First published 2000 by Walker Books Ltd
87 Vauxhall Walk, London SE11 5HJ

1 2 3 4 5 6 7 8 9 10

© 2000 Martin Handford
Consultant: Chris Gravett

This book has been typeset in Optima.

Printed in Hong Kong

British Library Cataloguing in Publication Data
A catalogue record for this book is
available from the British Library.
ISBN 0-7445-7757-8